Rebel Voices

EVE LLOYD KNIGHT   LOUISE KAY STEWART

wren
& rook

4
REBEL WOMEN

8
AUSTRALIA

16
CANADA

24
FRANCE

12
RUSSIA

20
ECUADOR

6
NEW ZEALAND

14
UNITED KINGDOM

10
NORDIC COUNTRIES

18
USA

22
SOUTH AFRICA

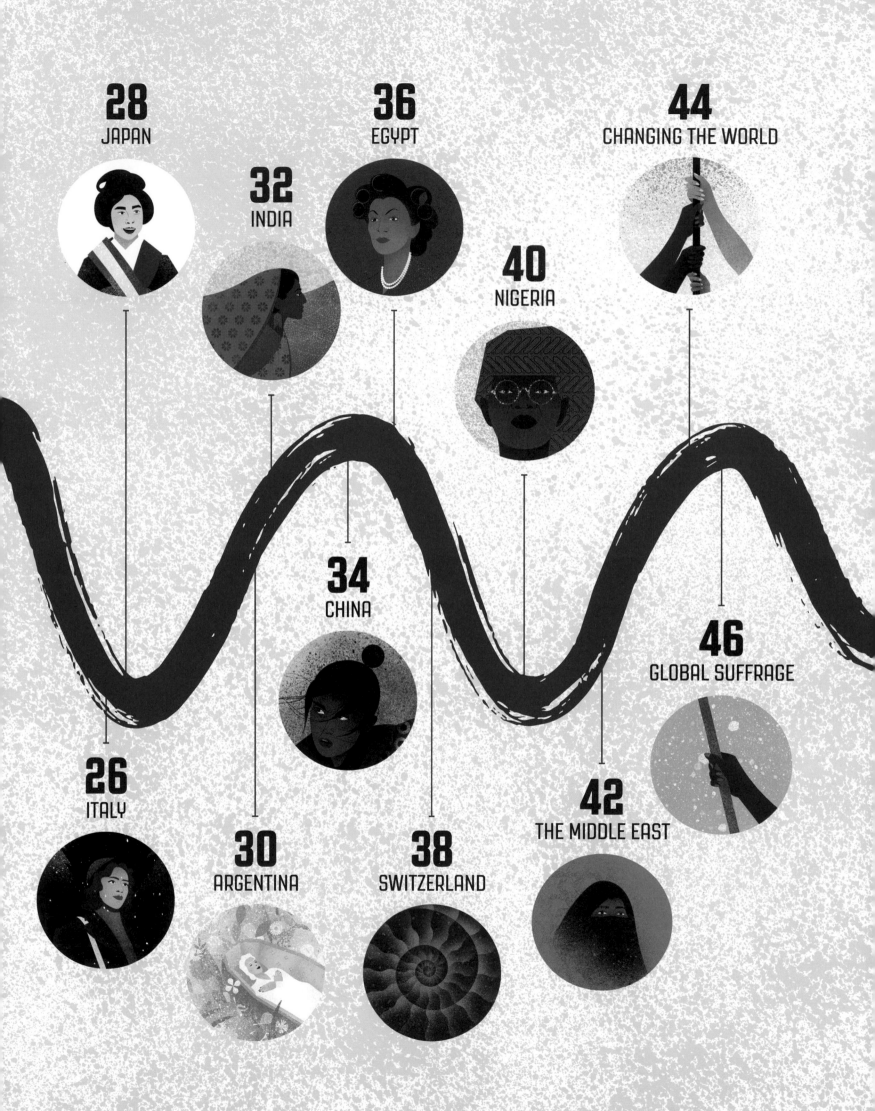

28
JAPAN

32
INDIA

36
EGYPT

44
CHANGING THE WORLD

40
NIGERIA

34
CHINA

46
GLOBAL SUFFRAGE

26
ITALY

30
ARGENTINA

38
SWITZERLAND

42
THE MIDDLE EAST

'WE'RE NOT DAUGHTERS, NOT WIVES … WE'RE HUMANS, WITH LIVES,'

sang a female voter during the 2016 presidential election in the USA. For more than 100 years, women all over the world have been fighting for equality and the right to vote. And it's a battle that continues today.

For centuries, women could only watch as men strolled to the polling stations to cast their votes. They were left at home, cleaning, cooking and caring for children, or toiling in fields and factories. Without the right to vote, women had no say in making the rules and laws that affected their lives. Men decided everything.

By the end of the 19th century, women could stay silent and powerless no longer. Suffragists from every corner of the globe began to fight, march, riot and petition for their voices to be heard. At first, their efforts were in vain. But slowly, little by little, a sea of change began to make waves around the world. When women in one country won the vote, they inspired, encouraged and actively helped their sisters in other nations to win equality, too. And so, bit by bit, step by step, they won their battles.

It wasn't easy. Women and the male supporters who fought alongside them for the vote faced insults, rejection, imprisonment and even physical attacks. Many were robbed of their livelihoods, their families and some even of their lives, as they struggled to secure equal rights. In a large number of countries, it took decades of wrangling before their efforts paid off.

The story of their struggle is one of courage and determination, teamwork and solidarity and, ultimately, survival and success. Every time a modern woman votes – whatever and wherever the election – she has her suffragist sisters to thank. These are their stories.

THE TRAILBLAZERS

Women around the world had been fighting for a voice and a vote for many years. But it was the expectation-defying frontier women who worked the wild, rugged land as hard as men, or fought alongside them to free their country from foreign rule, who kick-started everything.

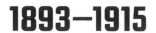

New Zealand

1893

Heads turned as Kate Sheppard sped through the streets of Christchurch, New Zealand on a bike in 1892. People thought that exercise like this could damage fragile women, so they discouraged the unladylike behaviour. But cycling gave Kate and her friends independence when most women weren't allowed to own property, or have an education or a career.

Kate's family had travelled to New Zealand from Britain, along with thousands of other settlers, during the 1850s. Life was hard in this tough, new land, and women worked alongside men building homes and tending farms. Because they were working as equals, women wanted to be treated as equals, and this included being allowed to vote.

To raise support for their cause, women published pamphlets, collected petitions and lobbied politicians. Kate travelled the country giving empowering speeches that drowned out any opposition. In 1893, history was made when both indigenous Maori women and female European settlers became the first women in the world to win the right to vote in a national election. Their success started a ripple that turned into a wave that began to spread around the world.

Australia

1902

The waves of change from New Zealand soon lapped at the shores of nearby Australia, another country full of adventurous European settlers who had braved long voyages to start new lives on the other side of the world.

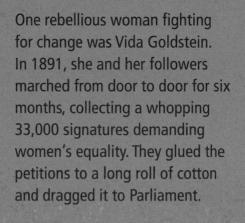

One rebellious woman fighting for change was Vida Goldstein. In 1891, she and her followers marched from door to door for six months, collecting a whopping 33,000 signatures demanding women's equality. They glued the petitions to a long roll of cotton and dragged it to Parliament.

Male politicians gasped in surprise as the 260-metre-long petition – the largest Australia had ever seen – was ceremoniously unrolled.

In spite of this triumph, it took 10 more years of political wrangling before Vida and the women of Australia celebrated winning both the vote and the right to run for Parliament.

Their victory in Australia inspired Vida and other suffragists to travel to the UK and the USA to campaign with their suffrage sisters for the vote.

Voting rights were only skin deep, though. Unlike in New Zealand, Australian Aboriginal women and men didn't get the vote until 1962, 60 years later. Sadly, Australia wasn't the only place in the world to grant women the right to vote, but deny it to minorities.

Nordic Countries

1913-1915

As congratulations poured in to New Zealand and Australia, rebel voices in another corner of the globe were determined to be heard. As each Nordic country broke free from the grip of foreign rule, women seized their chance.

Even the cold wind couldn't wipe the smile of satisfaction from Norwegian Gina Krog's face. She was one of the first women in the world to summit a mountain – at a time when ladies weren't even encouraged to set foot in a restaurant alone. Fired up by the British suffragists she had seen while studying in the UK, Gina set her sights on securing Norwegian women the vote. After years of writing articles, organising protest groups and struggling to be heard, on 11 June 1913 she conquered this obstacle as well.

The women of Denmark followed the lead of their Antipodean sisters and, in 1887, collected 20,000 signatures from women who wanted their say. The cause was hard fought and it took another 28 years, but on 5 June 1915, 12,000 women dressed in white flooded the streets of Copenhagen to celebrate winning the vote.

Instead of climbing a mountain, Briet Bjarnhedinsdottir mounted her horse and raced across the snowy paths of Iceland. She travelled day after day inspiring women to join her suffrage crusade, and only jumped out of the saddle on 19 June 1915 when the vote was won.

11

WOMEN AT WAR

Over the next 30 years, the world, and women, went to war. Firebrand feminists toiled and fought for their countries in revolutions and world conflicts, facing hardship and horror as bravely as any man. They also engaged in battles on the home front – marching, protesting and using any means in their power to combat inequality and win the right to vote.

Russia

1917

Grey, foreboding skies didn't deter the peasant women jostling eagerly through crowds to join the procession marching down St Petersburg's streets on 19 March 1917. Heads wrapped tightly in plain headscarves, they mingled freely with wealthy sister-protesters in extravagant fur and feather hats.

Soon there was an army of 40,000 determined women advancing towards the Russian Parliament. Pausing only to pose and smile for bystanders' cameras, arms aching from the effort of holding banners, the demonstrators pressed onwards. Leading the procession were female guards astride white horses, fresh from fighting in Russia's violent revolutions. Spectators cheered as rebel leader Vera Figner waved from an open-top car, and two orchestras gave the procession a carnival atmosphere.

The march came to a halt outside Parliament, surrounding the building while a troop of women, including Vera Figner, confronted politicians inside. At first, their demands met with stony-faced disapproval, but the women refused to leave, even after dark, when they were soaked by heavy rains and knee-deep in puddles. There were simply too many of them to ignore, and at last the government gave in. A triumphant roar went up through the crowd — victory was theirs! Russian women had won the vote.

Throughout the 19th century, suffragists in the UK protested peacefully, inspiring women worldwide. But by the early 1900s, they still had not won the vote. Enraged by the lack of progress, some rebel women decided that extreme action was the only way to make their voices heard.

United Kingdom

1918

Emmeline Pankhurst and her followers were the vanguard of a new kind of British army. They wore 'Votes for Women' sashes like battle dress and marched to huge, noisy rallies. They attempted to invade Parliament, and to force their way into Buckingham Palace to appeal directly to the King. They also took guerrilla action to grab attention for their cause. Pulling hidden hammers from their flowing skirts, they smashed hundreds of windows, set post boxes ablaze and started riots. Reporting on their hell-raising acts of disruption, one newspaper sneeringly dubbed them 'suffragettes'. The rebels embraced this new name – ensuring the attempt to denigrate them as second-class suffragists failed.

The suffragettes suffered for their actions. Beaten in violent clashes with police, many bruised and bloodied protesters were strong-armed into vans and dumped in prisons. Jailed suffragettes protested by refusing to eat, but were brutally and repeatedly force-fed by guards through long plastic tubes. Some never recovered from their ordeal. In the end, though, the ill-treatment backfired, and won the suffering suffragettes welcome publicity and sympathy.

When the First World War broke out in 1914, the suffragettes put their protests on hold.

Women set aside their sashes to drive trams, build weapons, dig in coal mines and take over many other jobs left vacant by men who'd enlisted. Their stout-hearted efforts torpedoed any claims they weren't equal to men. When the war ended in 1918, women were granted the vote at last.

Canada

1918

The long, lavish curtains parted to reveal a noisy mock Parliament on the theatre stage in Winnipeg, Canada. In a cheeky role reversal, the Parliament was made up of women with high-profile suffragists acting as ministers. A group of men with a wheelbarrow full of petitions arrived on stage, pleading for their right to vote. Nellie McClung rose to answer them.

Nellie was in character as the Canadian premier and set about mocking and mimicking one of his real speeches. To cheers of delight from the audience, Nellie scoffed that men would waste the votes, that their place was on the farm and that giving them the vote would unsettle the family and the home. She even jokingly complimented them on their looks! The theatre rocked with laughter – the show was a sensation.

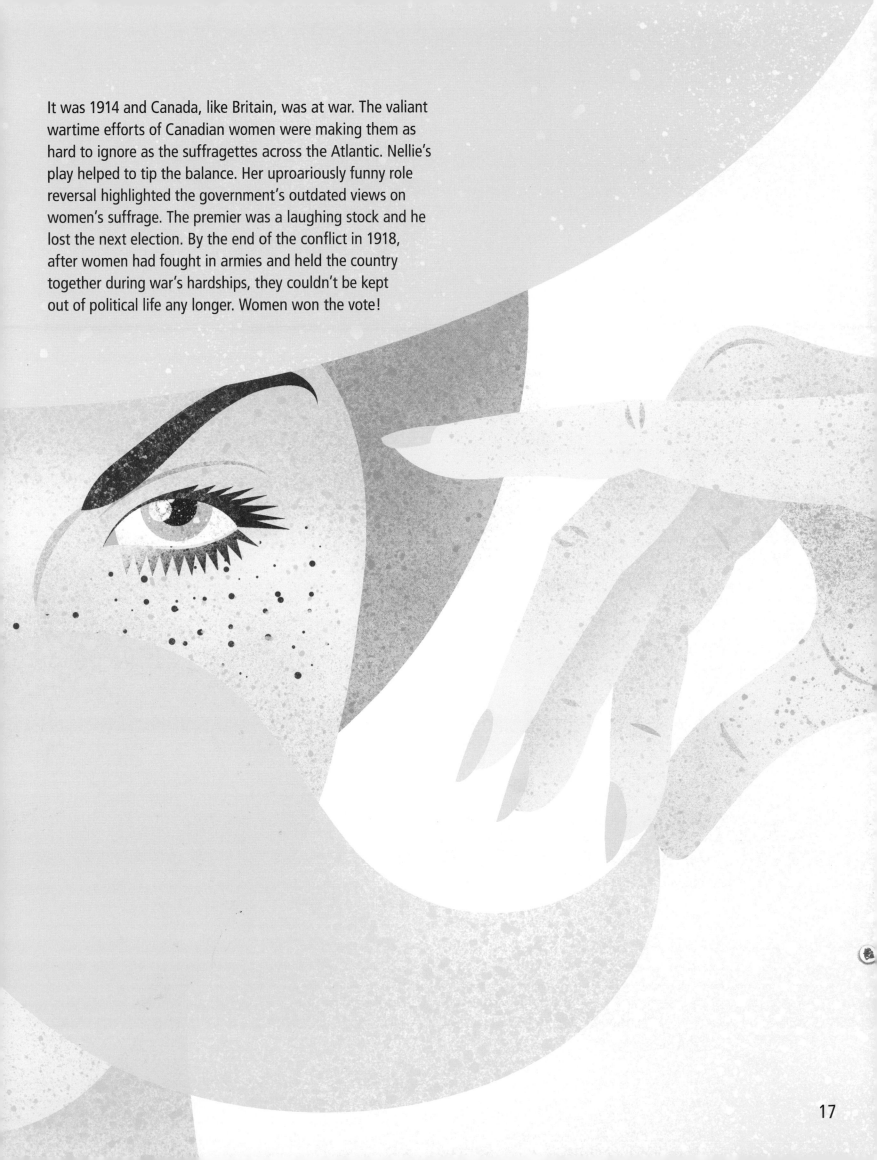

It was 1914 and Canada, like Britain, was at war. The valiant wartime efforts of Canadian women were making them as hard to ignore as the suffragettes across the Atlantic. Nellie's play helped to tip the balance. Her uproariously funny role reversal highlighted the government's outdated views on women's suffrage. The premier was a laughing stock and he lost the next election. By the end of the conflict in 1918, after women had fought in armies and held the country together during war's hardships, they couldn't be kept out of political life any longer. Women won the vote!

At six feet tall, Sojourner Truth towered above her audience. Speaking in Ohio in 1851, her powerful voice held listeners like a magnet as she half-spoke, half-sang a sermon supporting women's suffrage and denouncing slavery. Sojourner Truth was a name she'd chosen herself after becoming free. It steeled her on her long journeys across America, to spread her message to hundreds of listeners.

USA

1920-1965

Stirring speeches from charismatic feminists like Sojourner persuaded others to enlist in the suffragist struggle. In 1866, angry women filled New York's harbourside in protest when the Statue of Liberty was unveiled. They were furious that a female statue was to be an icon of freedom, when they had no freedom to vote.

In 1872, US feminist Susan Anthony argued officials into letting her vote in a presidential election. Susan was arrested and failed to persuade the jury that women had a right to vote, yet her trial made front-page news. Women hadn't won the war, but they'd publicised their cause.

In 1917 Alice Paul, later to become the leader of the National Women's Party, led a team of banner-waving suffragists in a silent vigil outside the White House. This quiet rebellion lasted more than two years. The authorities tried to stop these very public demonstrations from dominating the news by throwing the suffragists in jail.

When the violently beaten, force-fed and brutalised suffragists were released, many were too weak to walk on their own. Yet they donned prison uniforms and travelled the USA, giving rousing speeches about their injustices to increasingly large crowds.

The tide of public opinion turned in the suffragists' favour and in 1920, 8 million white American women voted in a presidential election for the first time in their lives.

Sadly, though, their African-American sisters faced a further battle, as discriminatory practices in many states prevented them from voting. They had to wait until 1965, when pressure from the Civil Rights Movement led President Johnson to make reforms, before they could freely exercise their right to vote.

1929

Ecuador

Whilst many women battled for years to alter outdated voting laws in America, it was the fearless actions of a single courageous challenger that provoked change in Ecuador.

Matilde Hidalgo de Procel was a small girl with big ambitions. Branded a troublemaker from a young age, Matilde sparked her first scandal when she persuaded the director of her local high school to offer her a place – a privilege until then enjoyed only by boys. Horrified mothers banned their daughters from befriending her and Matilde braved a daily gauntlet of insults on her way to school. Even her local priest tried to humiliate her

into submission by making her listen to services two paces outside the church door.

These cruel attacks wounded Matilde, but also drove her on. She became the first female doctor in Ecuador, and aspired to open doors for other women too. Her chance came when she discovered that although no woman had ever voted in Ecuador, it was not actually illegal for them to do so. Walking tall, she entered a polling station in 1924, sweeping past outraged officials who could do nothing to stop her. As she made her mark, Matilde gained another first – she was the first woman to vote in a general election in the whole of South America.

She had broken down the barrier keeping politics and women apart. By 1929, all Ecuadorian women could follow the intrepid Matilde into the polling station.

South Africa

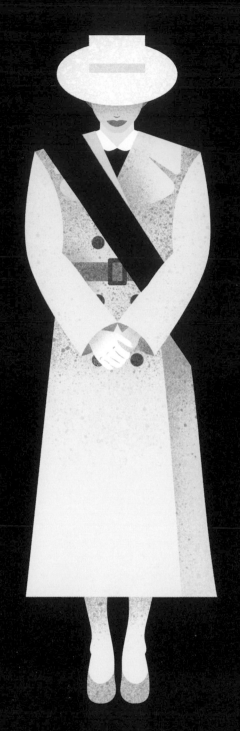

In Ecuador it was hard enough for women to win equality. But in South Africa's two-tiered society, where white European settlers ruled a black majority, the struggle to secure the vote for all was even more difficult.

When white South African women were granted the vote by an all-white, all-male government in 1930, many of them celebrated this long-awaited victory. Certain of their superiority, they even supported fresh laws to suppress the black men and women who worked in their homes and fields. But other white women were ashamed of the result, and marched and demonstrated in support of their black sisters and brothers. One group of white rebel women known as the Black Sash stood in powerful, silent protests in prominent places. They wore wide black sashes mourning the death of equal rights.

1994

On 9 August 1956, members of the Black Sash joined an historic march against the unfair laws that divided South African society. 20,000 angry women came from far and wide to raise their arms and voices in protest against the political chains that bound them. After handing the government hefty petitions containing 100,000 signatures, this vast community of women stood in compelling, absolute silence for half an hour, before breaking into a thundering song of defiance: 'Now you have touched the women you have struck a rock. You have dislodged a boulder. You will be crushed!'

The Women's March was a spectacular success, but protesters needed the strength of a rock or boulder to endure the tough years of riots, violence, arrests and beatings that lay ahead of them. At last, in 1994, black men and women were granted the right to vote. Today, 9 August is a national holiday in South Africa to remember and honour women's valiant efforts to create a fairer society.

Cameras began clicking the moment Marguerite Durand left her Parisian house with a majestic lioness in tow. It was 1910, and pedestrians gazed in open-mouthed astonishment as she paraded her unusual pet through the bustling streets, dressed in the latest eye-catching fashions. Durand's stunt made front-page news and gave her the chance to promote women's suffrage and spread the word about injustice. French suffragists knew that getting into the news could win them attention and support.

In spite of the suffragists' best efforts, many French traditionalists still held on to the idea promoted by one government advisor that women's hands were not 'for holding ballot boxes, but for kisses'. In the end, it was women's lionhearted efforts in the French Resistance during the Second World War, fighting bravely against the Nazi German occupation of their country, which finally made the difference. At last, in 1944, the real lionesses of France won their right to vote.

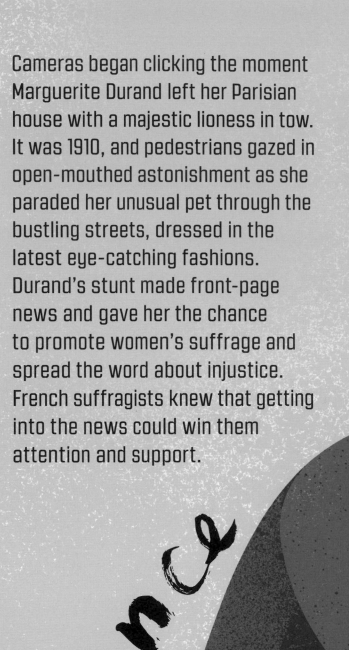

France

1944

Italy

A noise disturbed Ada Gobetti and she cautiously put down her pen to listen. Silence once more. Reassured, Ada returned to the notebook she used to record her daring activities as part of the Italian Resistance to the Nazi Occupation during the Second World War. Ada and her comrades smuggled weapons and explosives through dense mountain forests and carried messages across enemy lines under the watchful eyes of armed guards.

But tonight, wielding a machine gun under a sky full of stars, Ada and her team had derailed an enemy train. By preventing the Nazis carrying equipment across France, she helped to stop them extending their power. Ada frowned slightly as she carefully translated her latest escapade into the secret code she always used. She knew that if her notebook was ever found and the code deciphered, she would be executed immediately ...

Ada was one of many heroines who risked their lives for their cause during the Second World War. Some even fearlessly led troops of skilled resistance fighters into deadly battles against their enemy occupiers. In Italy, as in France, women's courageous fight to liberate their country from Nazi German occupation helped them to win the vote. In resisting, women also defied the stereotypes that confined them to the home and in 1945, they were finally granted the vote.

Before 1945, Japanese women had even fewer rights than women in France and Italy. They were expected to keep to the home and to walk three paces behind their husbands when they ventured outside. Women like actress and activist Kimura Komako ignored such restrictions. In 1917, she dressed in her finest kimono and marched proudly alongside 20,000 people in New York, USA, to demand that women everywhere get the vote.

Her presence at the march caused a sensation in Japan. After sharing ideas with enthusiastic American suffragists, Kimura Komako returned home. In Japan, her fame and inspiring feminist magazine named *Shin Shin Fujin* (New Real Women) brought publicity to the cause, and inspired other women to join the Japanese suffrage movement.

While Kimura made headlines, famous feminist Fusae Ichikawa made other breakthroughs, giving rebellious talks that spread the message of equality from village to village like wildfire. She never gave up, even when an angry man tried to drag her from a stage in 1931 in an ugly attempt to silence her. Even during the Second World War, when the government insisted women's place was in the home whilst encouraging them to work in factories, and suffrage groups were largely forgotten about, Fusae fought on.

After the war, when the USA occupied Japan, Fusae Ichikawa seized the opportunity to effect change. Using wise words and her powers of persuasion, she convinced American General MacArthur to finally give Japanese women the vote.

CATALYSTS FOR CHANGE

In the first half of the 20th century, wars had often been the impetus for change. But other kinds of upheaval helped women to win the vote by the millennium's end. Charismatic and courageous feminists were often instrumental in sparking these changes and when new governments came to power or a country was liberated from foreign control, women seized the moment and the right to vote.

Argentina

1947

Eva Perón made a great effort to lift her weary, cancer-ridden body up from the bed. Nothing, not even a fatal illness, could stop her today. The date was 11 November 1951. Four years earlier, Eva had achieved her dream of winning Argentinian women the right to go to the polls. This would be her first and last chance to join them in casting her vote.

Many Argentinian suffragists before Eva had fought long and hard for the vote, setting up mock elections and collecting petitions. But Eva made it happen. She had fought for this vote as she had for everything else in her life, working her way up from humble beginnings to become an actress and then helping her husband, Juan Perón, to become the president of Argentina. She worked non-stop, organising meetings and speaking passionately on the radio to win support for Juan and for women's right to vote.

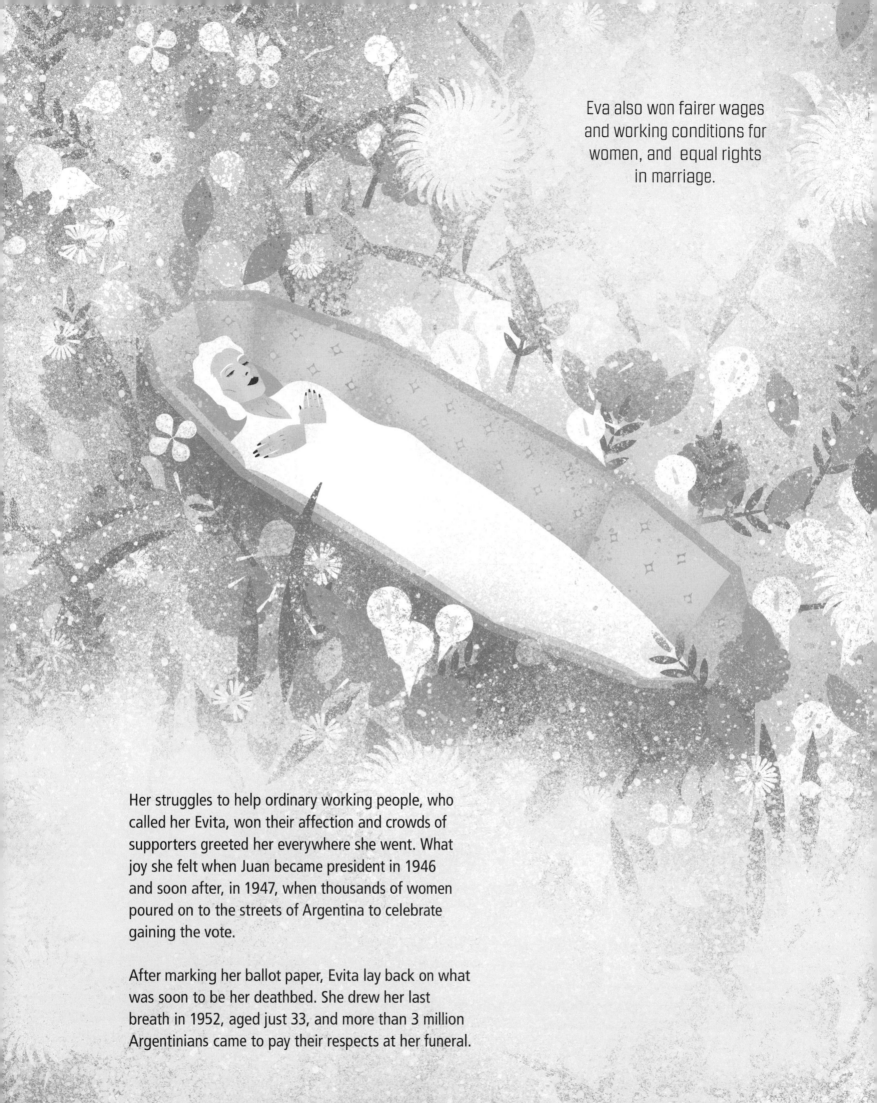

Eva also won fairer wages and working conditions for women, and equal rights in marriage.

Her struggles to help ordinary working people, who called her Evita, won their affection and crowds of supporters greeted her everywhere she went. What joy she felt when Juan became president in 1946 and soon after, in 1947, when thousands of women poured on to the streets of Argentina to celebrate gaining the vote.

After marking her ballot paper, Evita lay back on what was soon to be her deathbed. She drew her last breath in 1952, aged just 33, and more than 3 million Argentinians came to pay their respects at her funeral.

India 1949

Lifting their colourful sari hems from the dusty streets, Princess Sophia Duleep Singh and the other Indian feminists sidestepped potholes as they joined British suffragettes in a crowded march through London, UK in 1911. When she was a child, Sophia had watched leopards and cheetahs pacing in cages in her garden. Now it was her mission to free women from the confines that held them back and limited their lives.

India at this time was under British rule and, just as Argentinian women only won the vote after a change of government, Indian women had to wait for a political sea change to be empowered, too.

Back in India, Sophia's infectious enthusiasm inspired Herabai and Mithan Tata to join the struggle. Mother and daughter worked tirelessly to persuade UK leaders to give Indian women the vote, and to win support from their British suffragist sisters. From a young age, Mithan had devoured books by English feminist Annie Besant, so she bristled with pride when she stood to address MPs in London alongside Besant and Indian feminist Sarojini Naidu.

Sarojini Naidu was known as the Nightingale of India because of her lyrical poetry and she had a gift for expressing big ideas in powerful, creative ways. Her passionate speeches persuaded thousands in India to fight for both Indian independence and women's suffrage. Finally, in 1945, India cast off the shackles of British rule and in 1949, when a new constitution was signed for the liberated country, Indian women got the full and equal voting rights they deserved.

China 1949

The women of India used speeches and demonstrations to win the vote. But some feminists in China drew inspiration from rebel British suffragettes and militant heroines of their own, like the legendary sword-wielding Mulan who disguised herself as a male warrior to win glory on the battlefield.

When she was young, Tang Qunying had adored stories of Mulan and, like her daredevil idol, she too was a fighter. An expert swordswoman, Tang led female soldiers into battle during a violent revolution to bring down a cruel emperor in 1911. Now she led female comrades in their struggles for women's rights.

Tang set up the first women's suffrage group and campaigned for girls to get an education. She also helped to win the crusade to ban foot binding – a cruel ancient practice in which girls' feet were tightly wrapped to bend and break them so they could be squashed into tiny 'dainty' shoes. Tang glanced down at her own small feet – they might be painfully bound but they could still run and kick. They would not slow her down today …

Raising a pistol in her hand and uttering a battle cry to rally the fearless women beside her, Tang and her comrades stormed into Parliament to demand to speak about women's suffrage in 1912. When they were refused, the rebel women were furious. They hurled a torrent of abuse,

smashed windows, and kicked a guard to the ground. Troops were called in to force the women to retreat.

Tang's militant tactics failed, but they inspired Chinese suffragists to ramp up their peaceful protests. Wars within their country, and the Second World War, delayed their progress. But in 1949, when a new government declared China a 'People's Republic', women won the vote.

Such was Tang's commitment to education, she also founded two girls' schools in Shanghai.

Egypt

1956

If China's warrior women were the natural heirs to Mulan, Egypt's suffragists surely inherited strength from their powerful past too. In ancient Egypt, a woman could only became Pharaoh, or ruler, in special circumstances, but otherwise women were equal to men and the warrior goddess of healing, Sekhmet, was even depicted as a lioness, the fiercest hunter. But by the 20th century, Egypt's lionesses no longer had equal status to men.

By 1951, fearless feminist Doria Shafik, leader of the Egyptian Feminist Union, had had enough. She and 1,500 other courageous women marched on the Egyptian Parliament, and her roar of defiance echoed around the world. The attack failed, but Doria did not give up, and in 1954, she took action again.

Doria and a small group of her supporters took over the offices of the Egyptian press and began a hunger strike, refusing all food. After eight days, Doria was weary. Her stomach rumbled and the face that greeted her in the mirror was thin and

gaunt. But she drew strength from the fact that photos of the group, starving but determined in hair rollers and dressing gowns, had captured the world's attention. When officials arrived to try to persuade the women to end their protest, Doria turned them away, sensing that victory was near.

She was right. With the eyes of the world upon it and pressure mounting, the newly elected government finally gave in. Ministers set out a new constitution in 1956, including women's right to vote.

The radical actions of feminists in some other countries made many people in conservative Switzerland think female suffrage was a dangerous threat to the traditional roles of women and men. Realising aggressive tactics could backfire and lose them support, Swiss suffragists in the 1960s focused on using their considerable powers of persuasion to win the vote.

1971

Switzerland

It was hard for suffragists to swallow their exasperation when they remembered how long they had been struggling for equal rights. As far back as 1928, their feminist forebears had paraded a model of a giant snail through the capital city's crowded streets as a symbol of their impatience with Switzerland's slow rate of change. But there was nothing for it. Every major change in a Swiss law required a referendum, so the only way to win the vote was to win the support of the men who voted.

The women talked to as many people as they could, even travelling to lonely mountain villages where they gently but forcefully persuaded their listeners that it was time to give women the equality they deserved.

In 1971, these same women waited tensely outside polling stations across the country while their male friends, partners and neighbours went to cast their votes on a new suffrage law. The majority voted in their favour and the wait was over at last. The power of persuasion had prevailed.

Nigeria
1976

Through her round-rimmed glasses, Funmilayo Ransome-Kuti's piercing eyes glared furiously at the guard brandishing the Oro stick and roaring threats. It was 1944, and Funmilayo had rallied female market traders in Egbaland to protest about the unfair taxes the town's ruler, the alake, imposed on them.

Now her followers faltered in fear: the Oro stick was a mighty symbol of male power and defying the guards could bring bullying, beatings and arrests. Raising herself up to her full height, Funmilayo rushed forwards and ripped the stick from the guard's grasp. Waving it defiantly in the air, she shouted that women now held the power in their hands. Emboldened, her followers swarmed forwards and the humiliated guards ran for cover.

Funmilayo's daring revolt helped to force the alake to stand down. Her success inspired her to fight not only to win women the vote, but also to free Nigeria from the British who ruled her country and controlled local leaders like the alake.

Funmilayo travelled tirelessly, giving fiery speeches all over Nigeria and in Britain. Many thousands of women and men responded to her call, but it proved to be a long, hard struggle. Nigeria became independent from Britain in 1960, but women had to wait until a sympathetic new government came to power in 1976, just two years before Funmilayo's death, to win the vote.

Funmilayo was also the first Nigerian woman to drive a car and ride a motorbike.

Qatar

In Qatar, politician Sheikha Al-Jufairi's fingers tapped quickly as her car glided down the palm-tree- and skyscraper-lined avenues of the capital Doha. Her Facebook and Twitter posts reached new voters and supporters every day and had helped her to become the first woman to win a council seat in the country. As her face, and those of other women in leadership roles, appeared on the country's screens more and more, Qatar woke up to the importance of women in shaping its future. In 2003, a new constitution formally enshrined women's right to vote.

2003

Kuwait

When Rola Dashti's mobile buzzed, she snatched it up and smiled. She organised protests for women's voting rights by sending messages to supporters across the country, and numbers were swelling. In 2005, this online activism helped her to plan a large, peaceful demonstration in front of Parliament. It was a huge success and in that same year Rola celebrated a double victory: not only did women win the right to vote, but she also became one of the first female MPs to be elected to the Kuwaiti Parliament.

2005

Saudi Arabia

With hands firmly gripping their steering wheels, the women nodded encouragement to each other through dusty windscreens. In 1990, 47 Saudi women drove in convoy around the capital city Riyadh, defying their country's ban on female motorists. Although they were arrested, sacked from their jobs and publicly shamed, their courageous action sparked the beginning of the women's suffrage movement in Saudi Arabia. It encouraged more women to raise their voices and demand change and eventually, it worked. In 2015, not only did women win the vote, but almost 1,000 stood as government candidates as well.

2015

LIKE A ROW OF DOMINOES, FALLING THROUGH HISTORY, BARRIERS TO EQUALITY TOPPLED AS ONE COUNTRY AFTER ANOTHER GRANTED WOMEN'S SUFFRAGE.

Winning the right to vote gave women a voice and a choice – and a chance to change their lives.

The last 100 years has seen a huge improvement in equal opportunities around the world. But not all the battles are won. Women still have less power, fewer rights and opportunities, lower pay, more limited access to education, and are often treated as less capable than men.

Women's suffrage is a brilliant example of what can be achieved when people pull together. Just as suffragists around the world supported each other, today women share advice and ideas via the Internet and social media. The fantastic feminists who fought for the vote inspired each other across borders and boundaries, and feminists today continue to inspire girls and women everywhere as they work to create a fairer, more equal world.

This timeline shows the dates when countries of the world granted women the vote.

1893 New Zealand

1902 Australia

1906 Finland

1913 Norway

1915 Denmark, Iceland

1917 Russia

1918 Austria, Canada, Germany, Hungary, Latvia, Lithuania, Poland, UK

1919 Belgium, Kenya, Luxembourg, Netherlands, Rhodesia (now Zimbabwe)

1920 Albania, Czechoslovakia (now the Czech Republic and Slovakia), USA

1921 Sweden

1922 Ireland

1923 Burma (now Myanmar)

1924 Mongolia

1929 Ecuador, Puerto Rico

1930 South Africa

1931 Ceylon (now Sri Lanka), Spain

1932 Brazil, Uruguay, Thailand

1934 Cuba, Turkey

1937 Philippines

1938 Bolivia

1939 El Salvador

1941 Panama

1942 Dominican Republic

1944 France, Jamaica

1945 Bulgaria, Guatemala, Italy, Japan, Senegal

1946 Cameroon, Djibouti, Democratic People's Republic of Korea, Liberia, Portugal, Romania, Trinidad and Tobago, Vietnam, former Yugoslavia

1947 — Argentina, Malta, Mauritius, Singapore, Venezuela

1948 — Israel, Republic of Korea, Seychelles, Suriname

1949 — Chile, China, Costa Rica, India, Indonesia, Syria

1950 — Barbados, Haiti

1951 — Antigua, Dominica, Grenada, Nepal, Saint Lucia, St Vincent and the Grenadines

1952 — Greece, St Kitts and Nevis

1953 — Guyana, Lebanon, Mexico, Taiwan

1955 — Ethiopia, Ghana, Honduras, Nicaragua, Peru

1956 — Benin, Cambodia, Central African Republic, Egypt, Gabon, Guinea, Ivory Coast, Laos, Madagascar, Mali, Niger, Pakistan, Toga, Upper Volta

1957 — Colombia, Malaysia

1958 — Algeria, Iraq, Chad

1959 — Morocco, Tunisia

1960 — Congo, Cyprus, Gambia, San Marino, Swaziland

1961 — Burundi, Mauritania, Paraguay, Rwanda, Sierra Leone

1962 — Bahamas, Monaco, Uganda

1963 — Iran, Mozambique, Somalia

1964 — Afghanistan, Belize, Libya, Maldives, Sudan (inc. South Sudan), Zambia, Tanzania

1967 — Yemen, Democratic Republic of the Congo

1971 — Bangladesh, Switzerland

1974 — Jordan

1976 — Nigeria

1990 — Western Samoa

2002 — Bahrain

2003 — Oman, Qatar

2005 — Kuwait

2006 — United Arab Emirates

2015 — Saudi Arabia

It also shows how suffrage often came in waves, sometimes at times of crisis and change. Many countries gave women the vote after a war, a revolution or when they became independent of foreign rule and wanted to forge a new identity.

INDEX

First published in Great Britain in
2018 by Wren & Rook

Copyright © Hodder and Stoughton, 2018
Illustration copyright © Eve Lloyd Knight, 2018
All rights reserved.

ISBN: 978 1 5263 0023 2
E-book ISBN: 978 1 5263 6089 2
10 9 8 7 6 5 4 3 2 1

MIX
Paper from
responsible sources
FSC® C104740

Wren & Rook
An imprint of
Hachette Children's Group
Part of Hodder & Stoughton
Carmelite House
50 Victoria Embankment
London EC4Y 0DZ
An Hachette UK Company
www.hachette.co.uk
www.hachettechildrens.co.uk

Publishing Director: Debbie Foy
Editors: Corinne Lucas and Elizabeth Brent
Designers: Eve Lloyd Knight and
Laura Hambleton

Printed in China